THE 306: DAY

Oliver Emanuel

THE 306: DAY

OBERON BOOKS
LONDON

WWW.OBERONBOOKS.COM

First published in 2017 by Oberon Books Ltd
521 Caledonian Road, London N7 9RH
Tel: +44 (0) 20 7607 3637 / Fax: +44 (0) 20 7607 3629
e-mail: info@oberonbooks.com
www.oberonbooks.com

A catalogue record for this book is available from the British
Library.

PB ISBN: 9781786821454
E ISBN: 9781786821461

Cover photo by Christopher Bowen

Cover design by Dill Design

for Matilda

Characters

NELLIE MURRAY

early twenties, from Glasgow, a munitions worker and peace activist.

MRS BYERS

early fifties, from Glasgow, the mother of Joseph Byers.

GERTRUDE FARR

mid-twenties, from London, widow of Harry Farr and mother to Gertie.

CASHIER

CUSTOMER

POST OFFICE MANAGER

AGGIE

HELEN

PRIVATE

GERTRUDE'S MOTHER

GERTRUDE'S SISTER

STEPHEN, *Nellie's husband.*

GETRUDE'S NEIGHBOUR

SHERIFF

PRISON WARDEN

SYLVIA PANKHURST

EDITH CAVELL

WPC CAMPAIGNER

ROSE ROSENBERG

CLARA GILBERT COLE

MRS PETHICK-LAWRENCE

ALICE WHEELDON

PASSER-BY

LADY ARKWRIGHT

JANET BOOTH

As well as members of the CROWD, MUNITIONETTES,
WIDOWS *and* POLICE OFFICERS.

<u>*Note:*</u> This play is a fiction inspired by real events and
based on the words of women who did exist. Any
factual errors are my own.

While it is not necessary to have seen or to know *The
306: Dawn*, this play follows the action of that story a
year on.

A dash (-) indicates an interruption.

An ellipsis (…) indicates a tailing away or a thought-pause.

An empty line marked … indicates an intention to speak.

Lines marked in bold are sung.

NELLIE, MRS BYERS and GERTRUDE.

ALL   **We are going forward.**

                    You can starve us
                    put us in prison
                    kill us
                    but no matter what you do
                    our voices
                    will be heard.

                    We will be heard.
                    We will be heard.

2.

Glasgow. 1917. Late afternoon. A public meeting outside a factory.

NELLIE MURRAY, early twenties, a munitions worker, is handing out leaflets. Her friend AGGIE is helping while HELEN, a tall woman with a length of wood in her hand, keeps an eye on the crowd.

NELLIE   Take one of these… Here… Pass them along will you? Ta… Everyone got one? Good stuff.

NELLIE steps up to address the crowd.

NELLIE   Ladies… and gents. Alright? Good to see you. Thanks for hanging about after a long day. I know a lot of you want to get away home so I won't take up more time than I have to.

A woman shouts from the back of the crowd.

CROWD 1   WHAT'S SHE SAYING?

NELLIE   Righty-oh. Hang on.

NELLIE turns over a box and stands on it.

NELLIE   That better? Can you hear me now?

Murmurs of ascent from the crowd.

NELLIE   How do you do. I'm Nellie. I work in this factory. Some of you know me, I'm sure. I'm here today to speak on behalf of the Women's Peace Crusade. What's that you ask? Well exactly what it says it is. Women fighting for peace.

The crowd shift and mutter.

NELLIE   I know, I know. Our government tell us we can't talk of peace. Not now. Not while our brave boys are fighting and dying across the Channel. They tell us we're fighting for justice, for liberty, that it's treason to say otherwise. But the government is lying. Aye. They are lying to each and every one of us. Once upon a time we were fighting to protect plucky Belgium, to save Europe from that bastard Kaiser Bill. But not anymore. This war is a war of aggression. This war is a war of Empire and it won't stop, no, not until every last man is face down dead in the mud of Flanders.

A few murmurs from the crowd.

NELLIE   So we must talk of peace now. It is time. Three long years it's been going on. Who amongst us has not suffered? Who has not lost someone near and dear? How much longer will this slaughter go on?

AGGIE claps.

AGGIE   Here here!

CROWD 2   SHAME ON YOU!

AGGIE   Here here!

CROWD 2   GET HER OFF. SHAME! SHAME!

CROWD 1   LET HER SPEAK!

The crowd argue with one another. NELLIE shouts above them.

NELLIE   But what can we do, you ask? How can the
                 likes of us make a difference? Let me tell you.

The crowd are quiet.

NELLIE   You'll all be aware of what's happening in
                 Russia, aye? A revolution. A new social
                 order. Universal suffrage. Peace. And tonight
                 we're lucky enough to have one of our sisters
                 come all the way from Moscow. Will you
                 fetch her in, our Helen?

*HELEN goes out before bringing in a plain Russian woman in
overalls and a cap.*

CROWD 2   BOO! SHAME! BOO!

CROWD 1   LET HER SPEAK!

CROWD 2   SHAME!

NELLIE   I'll tell you what's a shame, pal. It's a shame
                 that we've got a new Prime Minister that not a
                 single woman here could vote for. It's a shame
                 women have to do their men's work but
                 everything in the home as well. It's a shame
                 a woman's voice is ignored by a government
                 that only cares about its own power.

CROWD 2   BOO! BOO! TRAITOR!

NELLIE   Come up here and say that to my face.

CROWD 2   COWARD! FRITZ-LOVER!

NELLIE   Why don't you shut up for a minute? It won't
                 kill you. I'm here to tell you the truth, for
                 God's sake –

*A woman jumps from the crowd and attacks NELLIE but HELEN
knocks the woman back. A fight breaks out.*

3

NELLIE and the others make a run for it.

3.

MRS BYERS walks down the street. She's in her fifties, proper but shabbily dressed with wild hair.

She stops a PRIVATE in uniform.

MRS BYERS *(Clapping her hands.)* **It's you! It's really you! My darling boy, you've come back to me at last!**

The PRIVATE recoils.

MRS BYERS follows.

MRS BYERS Don't run away, Joe. Please. I want to hear all your news.

4.

London. GERTRUDE FARR stands at the front of the line at the post office. She's in her mid-twenties, working class. There's a long queue.

GERTRUDE is shaking her head, agitated.

GERTRUDE What? Say that again. I missed that. What did you say?

CASHIER I said there's nothing here.

GERTRUDE Nothing?

CASHIER No.

GERTRUDE Are you sure?

CASHIER Yes.

GERTRUDE But – but there must be. I – Have you got the right name? Mrs Gertrude Farr. Farr with two 'r's.

CASHIER   Yes I know you, Mrs Farr. You come in every week.

GERTRUDE   Exactly. I come in every week. Won't you check again, please?

CASHIER   *(Sighs.)* If I must.

The CASHIER looks through her chits.

CASHIER   No. I was right. There isn't anything for you this week.

GERTRUDE   How is that possible?

CASHIER   Search me. By rights you should be on the widow's pension. Didn't they send you a letter? Once the war office has been notified of a soldier's death, a note is passed to the army to stop the allowance and start the pension.

GERTRUDE   How do I find out about the pension?

CASHIER   Like I said, you should've had a letter.

GERTRUDE   I haven't received anything.

CASHIER   No?

GERTRUDE   No.

CASHIER   Well your name isn't on the list so there's very little I can do.

GERTRUDE   Can I see?

CASHIER   I'm afraid that's not permitted.

Another customer taps GERTRUDE on her shoulder.

CUSTOMER   Can you hurry along please, love? Some of us have things to do this week!

GERTRUDE ignores her. She leans forward to whisper to the cashier.

GERTRUDE   Look. I don't want to make a fuss but you've
                   made a mistake. My husband was in the 1st
                   West Yorkshires. He was killed last year. I
                   don't have a job. I have rent to pay. Our
                   daughter is three years old. I need money.
                   Today. If you can't help me, you better fetch
                   someone who can.

The CASHIER gives her a look before disappearing.

*A minute goes by. The queue is not happy. GERTRUDE stands her
ground and ignores the others' tuts and grunts.*

CUSTOMER   This bloody country is going to the dogs.
                   Nothing works. The post is terrible. I wrote
                   my lad a letter a week for three months
                   before they all came back to me in a big
                   bundle. They'd been sent to Coventry.
                   Coventry! I said what on earth were they
                   doing in Coventry? My lad's in France.

The CASHIER returns with the MANAGER.

MANAGER   Excuse me, Mrs Farr. Could you step out of
                   the queue?

GERTRUDE   What? Why? What's going on?

*The CASHIER smiles as the queue turn to watch GERTRUDE and
the manager.*

MANAGER   Mrs Farr. I regret that owing to the manner
                   in which your husband died, the office
                   has determined that neither you nor your
                   daughter is eligible for a pension. Your
                   account is now closed. I'd ask that in future
                   that you go to another post office and do not
                   bother our staff again. Good day.

*The MANAGER holds out GERTRUDE's account book. GERTRUDE
stares at it in the MANAGER's hand for a moment before taking it,*

*almost as if she doesn't recognise it. The other customers react. The
CASHIER spits under her breath.*

CASHIER   Fucking bitch.

*GERTRUDE exits slowly past the other customers – all eyes on her –
holding the account book in both hands. She keeps her head down.*

5.

The pub.

*NELLIE, AGGIE and HELEN are at a corner table with pints of beer.
At the next table, a PRIVATE reads a newspaper, occasionally stopping
to listen to the women.*

NELLIE   What's everyone so afraid of? How do they
                 stay quiet? Why aren't they bloody raging?
                 Don't make a fuss. That's the British way.
                 Keep your mouth shut and get on with it. I
                 could smack every last one of them around
                 the head.

AGGIE   Not exactly the action of a confirmed pacifist
                 if I may say so, Nellie.

NELLIE   Aye well. I can't help it. Some folk deserve a
                 good hiding.

AGGIE   I'll drink to that.

They raise their glasses. The PRIVATE smiles to himself.

NELLIE   That's three factories I've done now. Three.
                 Not once have I got to the end without a
                 fight breaking out.

AGGIE   What do you expect?

NELLIE   I expect folk to listen to sense.

AGGIE   You're too much of an optimist.

NELLIE   Am I?

AGGIE	You know you are. You believe that everyone wants what you want.
NELLIE	I believe people want an end to this endless fucking war, excuse my French.
AGGIE	Aye but they don't.
NELLIE	Don't be daft. 'Course they do.
AGGIE	They want to win.
NELLIE	What's the difference?
AGGIE	*(Smiles.)* All the difference in the world. Everything – newspapers, ministers in Church, even biscuit tins – everything tells us that we must crush Fritz or risk being raped in our beds.
NELLIE	You really know how to cheer a lass up don't you, Aggie?
AGGIE	You know I'm right. Most folk believe what they're told. They don't like hearing that their government lied to them.
NELLIE	Well I'm not giving up that easy. The WPC are organising a march through the city in a few weeks. I know that if people see our numbers, how many are willing to stand up, unafraid, they'll have to wake up. You in?
AGGIE	I'll have to see… It's not always easy to get away from the kids…
NELLIE	Our Helen?

HELEN nods.

| NELLIE | Good girl. You don't say much, eh? But you're always there. Actions not words. Don't know what I'd do without you. |

HELEN smiles. They drink.

The PRIVATE turns a page of his newspaper.

AGGIE   You should be careful, Nellie. Once of these days you could get yourself into trouble.

NELLIE   *(Makes a face.)* I'd say we're all in trouble. This beer is off.

AGGIE   Be serious.

NELLIE   I am. This tastes like a dog's arse.

AGGIE   I'm talking about your position. What's the boss going to say when he hears about what you've been up to?

NELLIE   Wasn't planning on telling him.

AGGIE   Someone else might.

NELLIE   Who? You?

AGGIE   There are spies everywhere.

NELLIE   Spies?!

AGGIE   Ssshhhh.

NELLIE   How much have you had to drink?

AGGIE   Informers to the Ministry of Munitions.

NELLIE   You're daft.

AGGIE   No I'm serious. There are girls who get an extra bob a week for reporting any chat they overhear. Anything against the war or against the Ministry. They don't even need evidence. These lasses can say whatever they like and no one checks. Have you not noticed folk disappearing from the factory?

NELLIE   Disappearing?

She laughs.

| AGGIE | You can make fun of me but I'm telling you. There are people in that factory that could make trouble for you. |

NELLIE gives her a look.

NELLIE	You're very informed about all this, Aggie. What's your angle? Where do you get this stuff?
AGGIE	I hear things, that's all.
NELLIE	How's that?
AGGIE	My brother-in-law is police.
NELLIE	Bugger that. You can't trust the police. They're all lying bastards.
AGGIE	No he's alright. Tells me all sorts. Like did you know there are women police?
NELLIE	You and your fairy stories.
AGGIE	Truly.
NELLIE	Women police? Now I've heard it all…
AGGIE	They're new. Set up to keep order in the factories and see that women and children stay in line at home.
NELLIE	That's marvellous isn't it? Women police to keep women in line. Who needs Lloyd George putting us in our place when we do a good enough job on our own?
AGGIE	Don't you think it's a good idea? Progress and that. It can't go back to the way it was before can it?
NELLIE	That's what they want you to think.
AGGIE	They?

NELLIE	They. Them. Bloody men.
AGGIE	How?
NELLIE	So you'll fall into line and keep quiet.
AGGIE	Some say we'll get the vote when the war's over.
NELLIE	Who's the optimist now?

NELLIE shakes her head.

NELLIE	We can't survive on the crumbs men drop for us. A little bit here, a little bit there. We need to stop fighting ourselves, get organised, take what's rightfully ours. Women have been quiet too long. We have the power to end this war and effect change for the future if only we are brave enough to speak out. It's our silence that has let this war go on as long as it has. This moment, here, right now… this is our chance.

The PRIVATE puts down his newspaper and claps.

PRIVATE	That's a pretty song. Almost as pretty as the girl who's singing it.

NELLIE shakes her head.

NELLIE	How long did it take you to come up with that one?
PRIVATE	You can't blame a bloke for trying.
NELLIE	Can't I?
PRIVATE	*(Raises his hands.)* I surrender! I surrender! I'm on the side of the angels, same as you.
NELLIE	Not in that uniform, you're not.
PRIVATE	I'm open to persuasion. Why don't I buy you a drink and you can give me the speech in full?

NELLIE pulls a wedding ring from her pocket and holds it up.

NELLIE   No, ta. My husband doesn't approve of me
                 drinking with strange men.

PRIVATE   That's hardly fair. Tell me your name at least.

NELLIE ignores him. She finishes her pint and stands up.

NELLIE   Right. It's been a pleasure, ladies. I have to
                 get home.

AGGIE   How's your man?

NELLIE   Bearing up.

AGGIE   Have you been allowed to see him yet?

NELLIE   Next week, fingers crossed.

AGGIE   And your mother?

NELLIE shrugs.

NELLIE   Long story.

AGGIE   You can tell me on the walk home. I'll chum
                 you.

NELLIE turns to the PRIVATE.

NELLIE   Sorry, pal. Why don't you buy another pint
                 for our Helen? She never refuses a drink. But
                 be warned, she bites.

*HELEN waves her empty glass. The PRIVATE blinks in surprise.
NELLIE and AGGIE exit arm-in-arm, laughing.*

6.

The munitions workers in the factory.

MUNITIONETTES **We build bombs**
              for our brave boys.

              Ten hours a day –

eight in the morning til one –
with an hour for lunch
back again 'til six –
we work
we work
we work.

We build bombs
for our brave boys.

Steady hands –
steady on, girls –
you can lose a hand or an eye
if you don't take care
we work
we work
we work.

We build bombs
for our brave boys.

Back home
at night
our skin yellow
as yellow as canaries.
And it only makes it worse when
we wash
we wash
we wash.

We build bombs
for our brave boys.

Yesterday I saw a train come in with the
wounded.
So many…
How many?
I didn't know there were so many.

'It's fucking hell', they say.
'It's hell'.
'It's hell'.

We build bombs
for our brave boys.

7.

A teashop.

GERTRUDE is sitting at a table with her MOTHER and SISTER. A one-armed PRIVATE plays piano in the corner.

GERTRUDE has just finished speaking. Her SISTER stares at her. Her MOTHER shakes her head.

SISTER	How long have you known?
GERTRUDE	That's your first question?
SISTER	What?
GERTRUDE	I say that and you ask how long I've known?
SISTER	What should I say?
GERTRUDE	You could be more sympathetic. I'm so sorry, Gertrude. How terrible. What can I do? Is there anything you need?
SISTER	It's a perfectly reasonable question.
GERTRUDE	Is it?
SISTER	Yeah.
GERTRUDE	You're my sister, not the police.
MOTHER	I'm not sure it's seemly for a wounded soldier to be working in a teashop. The poor boy only has one arm. He's hardly able to play. It must be humiliating after all he's been through. Wouldn't it kinder if he was

being looked after at home or, I don't know, in an institution of some sort?

SISTER   Mother, are you hearing what Gertrude's telling us?

MOTHER   Of course I am. How can I not?

SISTER   How long?

GERTRUDE   I – since the beginning.

SISTER   What?

GERTRUDE   I've always known. From the day the letter came. The letter… telling me about Harry, that – that he died. The letter said, it said he'd been executed for cowardice.

SISTER   Did it actually say that word?

GERTRUDE   What word?

SISTER   *Executed.*

GERTRUDE   I – I don't remember. I think so, yeah…

SISTER   *Cowardice.*

MOTHER   Ssshhh. Please girls. Keep your voices down.

SISTER   But that was last year. You've known for a whole year and you didn't say? You let us believe that Harry died in a normal way –

GERTRUDE   Normal?

SISTER   You know what I mean.

GERTRUDE   *Normal?*

SISTER   Normal like a normal soldier… like in battle.

GERTRUDE   What do you know about battle? What the hell do you know about normal come to mention it?

MOTHER	Language!
GERTRUDE	It's not me, it's her. She's being a right –
MOTHER	We don't want everyone hearing –
SISTER	Then why are we in a bloody teashop surrounded by all these people? Why couldn't we meet at home?
MOTHER	Enough. I won't have it. You know I can't abide arguments.
GERTRUDE	I needed to tell you.
SISTER	But why didn't you tell us before?
GERTRUDE	**When I got** **the letter** **I pushed it down** **inside my blouse** **and** **shut my mouth –** **When I got** **the letter** **I pushed it down** **I pushed it down...** **there's nothing to say.** **When I got** **the letter** **I pushed it down –**
MOTHER	Does Gertie know?

GERTRUDE shakes her head.

SISTER	Quite right. You shouldn't tell her.
MOTHER	Absolutely not.
GERTRUDE	She's too little now but maybe one day –

MOTHER   No.

SISTER   Never.

MOTHER   You can never tell her, Gertrude. Imagine.
              Just imagine if it got out. She might tell
              someone else then where would you be?
              Where would any of us be?

GERTRUDE   Us?

MOTHER   This kind of thing stains not only you but
              anyone close to you. Family, friends. We
              could all be shamed.

SISTER   It could ruin us all.

MOTHER   Much better to say that he died like the rest.
              In the normal way.

GERTRUDE   But – but that's not the truth –

MOTHER   What good's the truth? The truth will leave
              you with nothing. It will completely blacken
              your future.

SISTER   Better for everyone if you keep your mouth
              shut.

MOTHER   Yes and you must promise, Gertrude,
              promise that we will never speak of this
              again.

Silence.

GERTRUDE nods, slightly.

GERTRUDE   They've stopped my money. Because of the
              way Harry – they say we're not eligible.
              I had a bit put away but that's all gone. I
              owe rent. I've no food left. There's nothing
              for Gertie's dinner. I – I don't even have a
              penny for this tea.

MOTHER and SISTER exchange a look.

Silence.

GERTRUDE   You know I'm not asking for myself.

MOTHER   …

GERTRUDE   A short loan. I'll pay you back you know I will I –

SISTER   …

A moment. GERTRUDE stands up.

GERTRUDE   Forget it. You needn't say another word.

GERTRUDE goes.

8.

A prison cell.

STEPHEN, a Conscientious Objector in his early thirties, is kneeling beside a half-finished wooden coffin. He has nails in one hand and a small hammer in the other. He is very thin. NELLIE stands by the door.

STEPHEN   They've set us to building coffins. Not for the dead. Oh no. These are for the *next* battle. See, they have to be ready. They can't wait until after the fighting because that will be too late. Christ! They're cynical bastards. We have to do three a day. There are a hundred men working seven days a week for a month making a total of almost nine thousand. How many prisons are there? My personal feelings aside, isn't there something disgusting about a government that knowingly plans the annihilation of a hundred thousand men?

NELLIE   You're not eating.

STEPHEN   I suppose the higher-ups think this kind of work will get us down, turn us against the cause, but actually I find it quite relaxing.

NELLIE	Stephen, they say you're not eating.
STEPHEN	I was always terrible with my hands. Well you know.
NELLIE	Why aren't you eating?
STEPHEN	I never knew one end of a hammer from the other. But I've got the knack of it. Screws say my coffins are the best in the block. I know I shouldn't boast but it's hard not to feel a little satisfaction in a job well done...
NELLIE	Stephen.
STEPHEN	I like the feel of the wood. The way the nails go in, just so. There's music to it.
NELLIE	Stephen.
STEPHEN	What?
NELLIE	Are you listening to me?
STEPHEN	Are you listening to *me*?

Slight pause.

NELLIE	The governor told me you're on hunger strike.
STEPHEN	You spoke to the governor?
NELLIE	Just now. He asked to see me.
STEPHEN	Did he?
NELLIE	Aye.
STEPHEN	You shouldn't have done that. What if one of the others saw you? They might think I was havering.
NELLIE	How could I refuse?
STEPHEN	Just... say no or don't come next time.

NELLIE   But – but I want to see you.

Silence.

STEPHEN doesn't look at her but nods. He gets back to work.

STEPHEN   What news?

NELLIE   Of the war?

STEPHEN   Bugger the war. What's happening in Russia?

NELLIE   The Provisional Government is promising to stay in the fight to keep Fritz busy on the Eastern Front but soldiers are deserting all over the shop. It can't last. Oh and Lenin is back in Moscow.

STEPHEN   Is he now? That will set the cat amongst those fat, lazy pigeons.

NELLIE   Get this. It was the Kaiser what got him there.

STEPHEN   Was it?

NELLIE   Put him on a sealed train from Zurich.

STEPHEN   A sealed train?

NELLIE   Aye of course the Kaiser loves the idea of revolution as long as it's not in his back yard. So Fritz gave Lenin safe passage but he wasn't allowed to get off the train to address the people or even stretch his legs.

STEPHEN   *(Laughs.)* Kaiser Bill's not as simple as he looks.

NELLIE   Well I don't know. There's a lot of folk that think once Russia goes red it won't be long until the whole edifice starts to crumble.

STEPHEN   We are building a new world, Nellie. Mark my words. I'll have to write this up for the newspaper.

NELLIE   Newspaper?

STEPHEN   Didn't I tell you?

NELLIE shakes her head. STEPHEN talks quietly.

STEPHEN   Aye a couple of us write a newspaper every month. On sheets of toilet paper. Just a single copy but it gets passed along to the other COs. I'm the editor. We've had five editions so far and the screws haven't cottoned on.

NELLIE   Isn't it dangerous? What if you're caught?

STEPHEN   It's just a bit of fun, eh?

They smile. A beat.

STEPHEN   And you? What's the news with you, Nellie Murray?

NELLIE   I'm alright.

STEPHEN   You look better than alright. You look good.

NELLIE   Do I?

STEPHEN   This factory work suits you. You're stronger. Healthier. Is it possible you've got taller?

NELLIE   'Course not, you idiot.

STEPHEN   When I get out, you can carry on working and I'll stay at home. I'll fix things. How does that sound?

NELLIE   Blissful.

STEPHEN   How's your mother?

NELLIE   The same.

STEPHEN	You should get her to see someone. A specialist.
NELLIE	Never mind about that. It's you I'm worried about.
STEPHEN	You shouldn't worry.
NELLIE	How not? A hunger strike?
STEPHEN	It's not just me. The whole block of COs. It's a statement. We will not be silenced.
NELLIE	But it's so dangerous.
STEPHEN	Don't scold me, woman. It's all I've got –

NELLIE raises her eyebrows.

NELLIE	How?
STEPHEN	You know what I mean –
NELLIE	No I don't.
STEPHEN	Nellie.
NELLIE	It's all you've got? What about me?
STEPHEN	Nellie.
NELLIE	I don't ask much of you as a husband, Stephen, but I do ask that you stay alive.
STEPHEN	You can't ask that.
NELLIE	I thought the one advantage of you being put away was that you'd at least survive.
STEPHEN	Those men in France have their war, this is mine.
NELLIE	Stephen.
STEPHEN	No, Nellie. I have to fight. If I don't, I can't live.

NELLIE   You won't live if you starve yourself.

STEPHEN looks down at his hands, the hammer and nails. His hands are shaking a little.

STEPHEN   Do you know what I'm afraid of? Not death. I'm so afraid of giving in. I could walk out of here tomorrow. All I'd have to do is knock on that door and say I'm ready to serve. Fuck. I know you're suffering and I'm the cause. I'm ashamed.

NELLIE   No.

STEPHEN   Aye.

NELLIE   No you're wrong.

STEPHEN   I'm not.

A beat.

NELLIE   I'm proud of you. I know what you're doing is for the good of everyone, the future –

A banging on the door. The warden calls out.

WARDEN   HURRY ALONG NOW. TIME'S UP.

NELLIE goes to STEPHEN, kneels and kisses him.

STEPHEN   You're the strong one, Nellie. You always were.

NELLIE   Nonsense.

STEPHEN   Look at you.

NELLIE   I hate leaving you here like this.

WARDEN   TIME. IT'S TIME.

STEPHEN nods at her.

STEPHEN   Go. Go. I have to be getting on. I'll see you, Nellie.

NELLIE gives him a look. STEPHEN returns to his work. She exits.

23

9.

A YOUNG, PREGNANT WOMAN stands at her front door, holding a letter.

YOUNG WOMAN **I found I was expecting**
not long after he went away.

I saw the postman on the street
I knew he was coming for me.

It was Monday morning when I got the
letter
I didn't have long to go.

I saw the postman on the street
I knew he was coming for me.

'Dear Mrs Morton, I'm sorry to tell you
etcetera etcetera etcetera'.

I saw the postman on the street
I knew he was coming for me.

Other WOMEN appear at their front doors, each holding a letter.

A POSTMAN walks slowly down the street.

10.

MRS BYERS stands on the doorstep, watching the postman. She is excited, hopeful.

MRS BYERS   Good morning. Is there anything for Byers?

The POSTMAN shakes his head, moves on.

She sighs and closes the front door.

11.

GERTRUDE's bedroom.

A NEIGHBOUR is sitting on the edge of the bed, cleaning her nails with a penknife. She wears a nurse's uniform.

GERTRUDE moves around the room, collecting items to pack in a small suitcase.

NEIGHBOUR   It's alright for married girls. They don't have to work. They can spend all day queuing. What about me eh? I was working at the hospital from six this morning 'til eight tonight, only half an hour for lunch. I ran to the grocers as they were shutting and asked for milk. I've had nothing for days and days. Do you know what the woman said to me? She said you can have the milk if you've got a kid. A kid? What? Should I get myself knocked up for pint of milk? I popped next door to the butchers as he was dolling out the last of the rations. Very slim pickings. I pointed to a bit of meat and said that looks like cat. He nodded and said it is. I said I was hungry but I wasn't that hungry.

GERTRUDE hasn't been listening.

NEIGHBOUR   Gertrude?

GERTRUDE   Sorry what was that?

NEIGHBOUR   Did you hear what I was saying? Were you listening?

GERTRUDE   Yeah. No. I feel a little –

She sways.

NEIGHBOUR   Are you alright? Stop running around for a second.

25

GERTRUDE   It's fine. Silly. Don't know what came over me. My head. The air in here's a bit thick. Do you mind if I open the window –

She moves to the window but the NEIGHBOUR takes her arm and steers her to the bed.

NEIGHBOUR   Not so fast. When was the last time you had something to eat?

GERTRUDE   Well er… I made Gertie some porridge this morning.

NEIGHBOUR   Not Gertie. You. When was your last meal?

She shrugs.

GERTRUDE   What day is it?

NEIGHBOUR   Thursday.

GERTRUDE   Yesterday. Or Tuesday. I forget exactly –

NEIGHBOUR   Why didn't you say anything? Here I was talking about shopping and there you are starving.

GERTRUDE   Honestly, I'm fine. Just tired.

NEIGHBOUR   You're a terrible liar, Gertrude.

GERTRUDE smiles.

GERTRUDE   The landlord came round this morning. He heard our money has stopped. He's kicking us out.

NEIGHBOUR   He never!

GERTRUDE   He is.

NEIGHBOUR   Bastard.

GERTRUDE   No I guessed it was coming.

NEIGHBOUR   Who does he think he is? I'll give him a
             piece of my mind. Chucking widows and
             orphans onto the street. Your husband died
             for this country.

GERTRUDE covers her mouth with her hand. A beat.

GERTRUDE   What else can he do? He's right. There's not
             a penny left.

NEIGHBOUR   So where are you going?

GERTRUDE   No idea. I can't work. I've already taken
             advantage of Mrs Walker next door too
             much. She's been babysitting for Gertie in
             the mornings.

GERTRUDE goes to the window, looks out.

GERTRUDE   I remember the day before Harry left. It was
             just like this. Bright. No clouds. We had such
             plans. Harry was going to come back from
             the war and build us a new house. Did I ever
             tell you he was a builder? Harry was going
             to build us a big house with ten rooms and
             a kid in every room. *(Laughs.)* You must be
             joking, I said. You'll have to get yourself a
             couple more wives if that's what you want.
             He laughed. Said that wasn't a bad idea. He
             could build a nice big attic to keep his spare
             wives. I slapped him for that.

She laughs.

GERTRUDE   Hard to believe the world has changed so
             much. It could be a thousand years ago…

She goes to the bed and closes the suitcase.

NEIGHBOUR   Do you want to come and spend a night at mine?

GERTRUDE   I can't ask that.

NEIGHBOUR   You're not asking. I'm offering. Where else
             are you going to go?

GERTRUDE shrugs.

NEIGHBOUR   Come on, Gertrude Don't be proud. You and
             Gertie can have my bed and I'll kip down on
             the floor. It's only 'til you get yourself fixed
             with something better.

GERTRUDE hesitates.

NEIGHBOUR   Let me take that. *(She takes the suitcase.).* I'll
             make tea when we get back. I pinched a
             couple of sausages from my sister. I swear it's
             not cat. Or any other domestic animal, for
             that matter.

*The NEIGHBOUR goes. GERTRUDE takes one last look around the
room.*

12.

*A PRIVATE, home on leave, looks out of his bedroom window. His WIFE
stands behind him.*

WIFE   **What's up, my love? Didn't you hear me
             calling you? Why aren't you talking?**

PRIVATE   …

WIFE   **Darling? Hello! Is there anybody there?**

PRIVATE   …

WIFE   **It's me, your wife! Boo.**

PRIVATE   …

WIFE   **Talk to me.**

PRIVATE   …

WIFE	**What are you looking at, silly boy? There's nothing out there and I'm stood right here.**
PRIVATE	…
WIFE	**Talk to me!**
PRIVATE	…
WIFE	**Are you crying? Are you crying, my love? Why are you crying? Please don't…**
PRIVATE	…
WIFE	**I'm getting sick of this. Barely a word in two days and it's not fair when you've only got a week of leave. What's the point in coming home if you aren't going to talk to me?**
PRIVATE	…
WIFE	**Talk to me.**
PRIVATE	…
WIFE	**Talk to me.**
PRIVATE	…
WIFE	**Talk to me, my love.**
PRIVATE	…
WIFE	**Darling, hello?**
PRIVATE	…
WIFE	…
PRIVATE	…

13.

NELLIE's bedroom. A single room with a stove and wardrobe. A tall stack of books.

She is exhausted after a long day. Her movements are heavy and slow. She closes the door behind her and locks it. She goes to the window, looks up and down the street, before closing the curtains. She takes off her coat and hangs it up. She goes to the stove in the corner of the room and lights it. She checks the kettle and puts it on to boil. She gets a cup from the bedside table, finds it dirty but decides to use it anyway. She spoons in half a spoon of tea and waits. Once the kettle is boiled, she pours in the water. She upends a milk bottle but there is nothing in there. She gives up and moves to the bed.

She sits on the edge of the bed, warming her hands with the tea. She remembers something. She reaches into her overall pocket and finds half a biscuit. She smiles in triumph. She dips it in the tea and takes a bite.

After a moment, NELLIE begins to cry. Only a little at first but then big, heaving sobs.

A sharp knock at the door.

NELLIE   Hello?

    She wipes her eyes and gets hold of herself.

NELLIE   Hello? Who's there?

POLICE 1   Open the door.

NELLIE   If that's you, Mrs Harris, I put the rent under your door last night.

POLICE 2   This is the police.

NELLIE   What? Is that you, Aggie?

    Another knock.

NELLIE   I'm too tired for games. Come back tomorrow eh?

POLICE 1   Open this door or we will knock it down.

NELLIE	What?
POLICE 2	You have ten seconds.

NELLIE hesitates before unlocking the door. Four POLICEWOMEN in identical long black cloaks and red-rimmed hats burst in and begin to search the room.

NELLIE is rocked on her heels.

NELLIE	What's going on? What do you want?
POLICE 1	Are you Nellie Murray?
NELLIE	Who are you?
POLICE 2	Answer the question.
NELLIE	I'll not answer anything until you tell me what you're doing in my bedroom.
POLICE 3	This is not your bedroom.
NELLIE	What?
POLICE 3	As an employee of the Ministry of Munitions, you, this bedroom and its contents are the property of the government.
NELLIE	Are you insane?
POLICE 4	We are here to question you and search for any illegal material you may possess.
NELLIE	On what grounds?
POLICE 4	Under the Defence of the Realm Act of 1914, no person shall by word of mouth or in writing spread reports likely to cause disaffection or alarm among any of His Majesty's forces or among the civilian population.
NELLIE	How does that give you the right to invade my bedroom?

POLICE 2	There are serious penalties for committing an offence of this nature.
NELLIE	You don't frighten me.
POLICE 1	Are you Eleanor Murray born Eleanor Byers on 11 August 1896 at the Royal Infirmary, Glasgow.
NELLIE	Who's asking?
POLICE 3	We are members of the Women's Police Service seconded to the Ministry of Munitions.
NELLIE	Stop kidding about.
POLICE 4	If you don't answer us honestly we are empowered to take you down to the station.
POLICE 3	What will your neighbours say if you're marched along the street in handcuffs?
NELLIE	You wouldn't dare.
POLICE 3	Wouldn't we?
POLICE 1	Can you confirm that you are Eleanor Murray?

NELLIE considers. Nods.

POLICE 1	Can you further confirm that you are a member of the so-called Women's Peace Crusade?
NELLIE	Aye what of it? Oi! Those are my clothes. What are you doing with my clothes? Get your filthy hands off.

One of the policewomen has been ransacking NELLIE's closet, chucking clothes on the bed. NELLIE picks them up.

POLICE 2	Are you the author of this leaflet?

The POLICEWOMAN holds up one of the leaflets from the public meeting. NELLIE shakes her head.

NELLIE	Never seen it before.
POLICE 2	Oh no?
NELLIE	No.
POLICE 3	That's unfortunate. You were seen handing out this leaflet at an unauthorised public meeting.
NELLIE	Seen? Who by?
POLICE 3	Witnesses.
NELLIE	Bloody lies.
POLICE 4	Can you prove it?
NELLIE	Not up to me to prove it. I know the law. If you want to arrest me, it's up to you to prove I was somewhere else.
POLICE 1	Evasion won't get you anywhere. Better to speak now before you get yourself into worse trouble. *(Turns to the others.)* Any sign of a typewriter?

The other POLICEWOMEN shake their heads.

POLICE 4	Where do you hide your typewriter?
NELLIE	*(Laughs.)* What? Why would I have a typewriter?
POLICE 4	Then who publishes your leaflets? Do they have a printing press? It's against the law to print this kind of material without a licence.
NELLIE	Didn't you hear me tell you I've nothing to do with any leaflet?

Another POLICEWOMAN holds out a photograph.

POLICE 1	Take a look at this photograph.

NELLIE	What about it?
POLICE 1	Do you recognise this woman?

NELLIE shakes her head.

POLICE 2	Are you certain?
NELLIE	Oh hang about. Is it Vesta Tilley? Or the Queen?
POLICE 4	This is no joke.
NELLIE	Are you sure? Seems pretty comical to me. Have you lot ever considered a career in Music Hall? You'd make a great bunch of clowns.
POLICE 1	Are you denying knowledge of this woman?
NELLIE	*(Shrugs.)* Who is she?
POLICE 1	A foreigner. Russian. She's a member of the Third Moscow Soviet, a well-known agitator and troublemaker.
POLICE 4	She gained admittance to this country illegally and has since spoken at many factory gates and trade union meetings. She purports to be a Russian pacifist. In fact, she is a German spy dedicated to fermenting discontent amongst the masses while promoting Bolshevism.
NELLIE	How can she be a German spy *and* promoting Bolshevism?
POLICE 1	A woman matching her description was seen in your company.
NELLIE	I think someone's been pulling your leg, pal…
POLICE 3	Вы говорите по-русски?
NELLIE	Eh?

POLICE 3	Для кого вы работаете?
NELLIE	What's that? That's not English is it?
POLICE 3	*Sprechen Sie Deutsch? Sie können die Wahrheit nicht verbergen.*
NELLIE	*(Articulating.)* I – HAVE – NO – IDEA – WHAT – YOU – ARE – SAYING.

The POLICEWOMEN give up their search.

POLICE 2	There's nothing here.
POLICE 1	Sure?
POLICE 4	Just clothes, books, newspapers, personal items. Nothing else.
POLICE 1	Were you warned that we were coming?
NELLIE	How many times do I have to say it? I've no idea what you're on about.
POLICE 2	We don't believe you.
NELLIE	That's your problem. Now you've finished making a mess are you going to tidy up?
POLICE 1	I'm afraid we're far from finished.

The POLICEWOMAN checks her notebook and flips through the pages.

POLICE 1	Tell us. Why did you change your name?
NELLIE	I got married.
POLICE 2	Your husband's name is Murray?
NELLIE	Are you the clever one? Is she the clever one?
POLICE 2	Answer the question.
NELLIE	My husband's name is Stephen Murray.
POLICE 3	Does he live here with you?

NELLIE	Does it look like it?
POLICE 3	Where is he? Is he on active service?
NELLIE	Not exactly…
POLICE 1	Explain.
NELLIE	He's in prison. He's a Conscientious Objector.

The POLICEWOMEN share a look.

POLICE 4	Are you a member of the Non-Conscription Fellowship yourself?
NELLIE	Of course.
POLICE 2	And so is your husband's incarceration the reason you hate the government?
NELLIE	I'm a grown woman, thank you very much. I can hate the government all by myself. I don't need my husband's permission.
POLICE 3	Ah. So you're a suffragette.
NELLIE	Like most right thinking women. Why? Aren't you?
POLICE 3	Absolutely not!
NELLIE	What a surprise…
POLICE 4	Which suffrage organisation are you a member of?
NELLIE	The Woman's Social and Political Union.
POLICE 4	Mrs Emmeline Pankhurt's group?
NELLIE	Aye but not any more.
POLICE 4	No?
NELLIE	I resigned once Mrs Pankhurst started handing out white feathers and shilling for the war.

POLICE 1	Are you plotting to kill Lloyd George?
NELLIE	I'm a pacifist. I don't want to kill anyone.
POLICE 1	But you do blame the Prime Minister for the continuation of the war?
NELLIE	I believe that the government's policy of all out victory to be wrong, that Lloyd George has the power to push for a negotiated peace but chooses not to.
POLICE 2	That is defeatism.
NELLIE	Is it defeatism to say this war is wrong?
POLICE 2	Certainly!
NELLIE	Well I'll keep saying it until people start hearing me. This is not a just war. I'll shout it out of my bedroom window if I have to. It's a free country. Or it used to be.

The POLICEWOMAN makes a note.

POLICE 1	How is it that a member of the Women's Peace Crusade works at a munitions factory? How do you square building bombs with your beliefs?
NELLIE	I've got steady hands.
POLICE 1	Beg your pardon.
NELLIE	To build bombs you need steady hands. I've got very steady hands.
POLICE 2	But you're shaking.
NELLIE	No I'm not. *(She puts her hands behind her back.)* And anyway, like I said. My husband's in prison, my mum's not well. I'll take the best job I can get.
POLICE 3	We don't believe you.

NELLIE	I don't really give a fuck what you believe.
POLICE 4	Mind your language.
POLICE 1	We believe you are an agent provocateur.
NELLIE	Mind *your* language.
POLICE 1	We believe you were sent into that factory to create mayhem and disaffection. Who pays you? Who's your contact at the German Embassy?
NELLIE	You're all completely cuckoo. That you'd even imagine… *(She shakes her head.)* Get out. I've had enough.
POLICE 2	We're not going anywhere.
NELLIE	How? You have no evidence to arrest me.

The POLICEWOMAN checks her notebook again.

POLICE 1	Says here that you have a brother.
NELLIE	…
POLICE 1	Is that true?
NELLIE	…
POLICE 1	Do you have a brother?
POLICE 2	Answer the question.
NELLIE	Get out.
POLICE 2	Answer the question.
NELLIE	I – I won't talk about it.
POLICE 1	What does it say here? Oh yes. Here it is. Byers, Joseph. 1st Royal Scots Fusiliers. Executed for desertion on 6 February 1915.
NELLIE	You bitch.

POLICE 3	A lack of moral fibre is obviously something that runs in the family.
NELLIE	I'll kill you.
POLICE 3	Did you hear that? She threatened me. Witnesses!

The POLICEWOMEN move in to arrest NELLIE. She pushes them away and a fight begins. NELLIE kicks out and punches but is overwhelmed.

| NELLIE | Fucking get off me! |

NELLIE is pulled from the room, kicking and screaming.

14.

The next morning. Sheriff's Court.

NELLIE stands before the SHERIFF, a POLICEWOMAN on either side of her. Her clothes are torn.

SHERIFF	**Mrs Eleanor Murray. You have been found guilty of attempting to spread disaffection in a time of war and furthermore of threatening the life of a policewoman whilst in pursuance of her duty. You are sentenced to three months' incarceration.**
NELLIE	Is it my turn? Can I speak?
SHERIFF	**Silence**.
NELLIE	But I have something to say. I need to tell the court exactly what –
SHERIFF	**Silence. You do not have the right to speak. Take her away.**
NELLIE	Hang about – you can't do that – you have to listen –

NELLIE is dragged away by the policewomen.

15.

NELLIE is taken along a long, dark stone corridor and into a bare room. She is told to strip. She takes off her coat and dress but leaves her underwear on. The female wardens tell her to strip once again but NELLIE refuses. One of the wardens grabs her arms whilst the other one rips her underwear from her. A bucket of water is thrown over her. NELLIE screams. A male doctor enters and examines NELLIE: her eyes, her teeth, arms, legs, anus and vagina. She is made to cough. Her teeth chatter and her body is numb. The doctor makes notes, nods at the wardens and exit. A sackcloth dress is handed to NELLIE and she dresses. She opens her mouth to speak but there are no words.

16.

NELLIE is taken to her cell. A bare bed and a bucket. It is very dark. There's only a sliver of daylight from a high window.

The door is slammed behind her and bolted.

She looks about her, her body shaking, her voice caught in her throat.

NELLIE	But – but – but you can't do this. I – I don't like the dark. P – please. You can't shut me up in here.

She bangs her fist against the door. A sob.

	My mum. Who's going to tell my mum? She won't know what's happened to me.
WARDEN	SILENCE.
NELLIE	Can you get a message to her?
WARDEN	IF WE HAVE TO COME DOWN THERE, THERE WILL BE TROUBLE.
NELLIE	Please – I – I – I'm begging you –
WARDEN	SILENCE.

NELLIE falls to her knees, gasping.

NELLIE   Bastards. Fucking – fucking bastards.

A moment. A WOMAN'S VOICE calls from the next door cell.

VOICE   Are you alright, love? Calm yourself.

NELLIE   Who – who's there?

VOICE   A friend.

WARDEN   SILENCE.

VOICE   Take heart, Nellie Murray. You're not alone.

NELLIE   What's that? How do you know my name...?

From the other cells along the corridor of the prison come the voices of other female resistors of the war. Their faces remain in shadow.

SYLVIA PANKHURST steps forward.

VOICE   Sylvia Pankhurst of the East London Federation of Suffragettes and editor of the *Women's Dreadnaught.*

SYLVIA   **Deep down**
                        beyond race or class
                        beyond need or instinct
                        we are all human beings...

                        We are all human beings.

EDITH CAVELL, executed for spying in France.

VOICE   Edith Cavell, nurse, executed for spying in France.

EDITH   **Patriotism is not enough**
                        it is not enough.
                        I must have no hatred toward anyone.

SYLVIA   **We are all human beings.**

VOICE	Members of the Women's Peace Crusade, Glasgow.
WPC	**War is a victory of force** **the defeat of reason** **the history of women's progress** **makes it plain** **that women have everything to gain** **from the victory of reason.**
EDITH	**Patriotism is not enough.**
SYLVIA	**We are all human beings.**

ROSE ROSENBURG of Bethnal Green, steps forward.

VOICE	Rose Rosenberg, concerned citizen of Bethnal Green.
ROSE	To the Editor of the Times. Sir. I've got an idea. What if, in the future, women refuse to take over men's work unless our Members of Parliament are released from their duties to fulfil *our* places? See how the Honourable Members like making dinner and putting out the washing –

CLARA GILBERT COLE, nurse and poet.

VOICE	Clara Gilbert Cole, nurse, poet and anarchist.
CLARA	**War won't pay!** **Stop the war!**
SYLVIA	**We are all human beings.**
EDITH	**Patriotism is not enough.**

MRS PETHICK-LAWRENCE.

VOICE	Mrs Pethick-Lawrence, suffragist and social worker.
MRS P-L	**The bedrock of humanity is motherhood.**

> **Women all over the world**
> **have one passion**
> **one vocation:**
> **the preservation of human life.**

SYLVIA **We are all human beings.**

ALICE WHEELDON.

VOICE Alice Wheeldon, anti-war campaigner, convicted of conspiracy to assassinate the Prime Minister, sentenced to ten years' hard labour.

ALICE **We will keep a'going**
We will keep a'going
and break before we bend
we will meet again.
The world is my country.

ALL **We will keep a'going**
and break before we bend
We will meet again.
The world is my country.
The world is my country.
The world is my country

WARDEN SILENCE.

17.

Glasgow Central Station.

MRS BYERS is at the ticket counter.

MRS BYERS **I'd like a ticket, please. To see my son.**
I'd like a ticket to wherever it is, he
happens to be. I want to go where he
is. I want to go to him. I don't care if it's
the Somme. I don't care if it's Verdun. I
don't care if it's Arras. I don't care if it's

Ypres. Let me go to Vimy Ridge. Let me go to Loos. Take me to Deville Wood. Let me get to Menin. I heard of a place called Neuve Chapelle – I don't care. I don't care. I'd like a ticket to see my son.

She holds open her purse.

MRS BYERS   Why are you looking at me like that? You can't stop me. I have the right, don't I?

She pulls flower petals instead of coins.

MRS BYERS   What? There must be some mistake, I –

18.

Three months later.

NELLIE steps out of the prison door, onto the street and into the daylight. It is too bright. She blinks, blinded for a moment. She is noticeably thinner and her clothes are filthy. She rubs her eyes before taking a few tentative steps.

When her eyes have grown accustomed to the light, NELLIE checks where she is before moving off with purpose.

19.

The next morning. The factory gates.

NELLIE is standing on the step, barring the way for AGGIE and HELEN. Her hands twitch and she moves from one foot to the other.

AGGIE   You look like shite.

NELLIE   Ta.

AGGIE   Seriously, Nellie. What happened? There's barely anything of you. You look like you've lost three stone and not slept in a month. When was the last time that hair saw a hairbrush?

NELLIE grins, running a hand through her hair.

NELLIE	That better?
AGGIE	Not much. When did you get out?
NELLIE	Yesterday.
AGGIE	Welcome home. You should have a good, long bath. Go on. Get home and have a bath why don't you?
NELLIE	You look good, Aggie. You too, our Helen. Missed you. Why didn't you come and visit? I expect you were busy, eh?

AGGIE and HELEN exchange a look.

AGGIE	That's right. We've been extremely busy. They closed Dennistoun so we got all their orders. Production has doubled in the last month.
NELLIE	Is that right?
AGGIE	Aye on account of the Big Push. News from France is we're going to break through the line any day now.
NELLIE	*(Scoffs.)* Ha! You don't believe that.
AGGIE	Don't I?
NELLIE	They've been saying the same thing for three years.
AGGIE	One day it's got to be true. Stands to reason.

NELLIE frowns and takes a step towards AGGIE. AGGIE steps back.

NELLIE	There's something different about you. What is it? Hang about. Your uniform. You've been promoted.
AGGIE	I have.

NELLIE	The new get up suits you. What are you now? Supervisor?
AGGIE	Forewoman. Or Foreman, as the boss insists on calling me.
NELLIE	Wow! That's bloody brilliant. How did you swing that?
AGGIE	I'd like to think it was down to my hard work and initiative. That I proved myself the superior to those around me. Truth is, the last of the men in our hut got called up so there was no one else.

NELLIE laughs.

NELLIE	I bet the boss bloody loved that.
AGGIE	Couldn't look me in the eye when he told me. Looked like he'd been crying.
NELLIE	Amazing!

A moment.

AGGIE	Been nice catching up. We have to get on. A foreman can't be late, you know. Best of luck.

AGGIE tries to step round her but NELLIE blocks her path.

NELLIE	What's the rush, Aggie? I wanted to tell yous about my plan.
AGGIE	Plan?
NELLIE	Aye well I had a lot of time to think when I was inside didn't I?
AGGIE	Oh aye?
NELLIE	The leaflets and speeches are all very well but what do they accomplish really? They might change a few minds but our message isn't loud enough. No one is listening.

AGGIE	Why don't you tell us another time? We're actually in a bit of a rush.
NELLIE	The first strike at a munitions factory.
AGGIE	How's that?
NELLIE	Imagine it. What would that tell the government? An entire munitions factory downing tools and saying enough is enough. No more. It would be more than a message, it would be a cry that could ripple out and change the whole course of the war.

Silence.

AGGIE	Have you cracked?
NELLIE	What?
AGGIE	*(Hushed.)* We could be put away for even talking about this. It's illegal to strike at a munitions factory.
NELLIE	So what? This whole war is illegal. Think, Aggie. Helen. We could lead the charge for peace. In your new position, you could really get us going. I know you're not one for big speeches but maybe if you let me, I could talk to everyone –

AGGIE looks at her.

AGGIE	You've no idea do you...?

NELLIE shakes her head, confused.

| AGGIE | The morning after you were arrested, the factory was raided by the police. They said the place was booby-trapped, that you were a saboteur and had planted incendiary devices. Didn't find anything but that didn't stop them ransacking the place. We all got interrogated. Everyone, right down to the |

girls in the canteen. They were pretty rough, especially on our Helen and me. Later the boss made a speech saying you were a German spy. He said you spiked the bombs you worked on, put sand in them, so that they blew up in the faces of our soldiers.

NELLIE   What? That's a lie.

AGGIE   Is it?

NELLIE   You know it is. You know me, Aggie.

AGGIE   I know you've got a conchy for a husband and a mad bitch for a mother. Maybe you wanted revenge –

NELLIE goes to AGGIE and knocks her to the floor. HELEN grabs her arm but NELLIE is possessed and shoves HELEN against the gate. AGGIE cries out, grabs at NELLIE's leg. NELLIE kicks her before punching HELEN in the face as she tries to attack from the other side. NELLIE is wild, unhinged and vicious. AGGIE is knocked aside, blood coming from her eye.

HELEN roars in rage and wrestles NELLIE to the ground. Kicking and punching and biting.

Eventually, they are both exhausted and lie panting, bloody and bruised. NELLIE raises a fist to knock HELEN one last time but HELEN cries out.

HELEN   Please, Nellie. Stop –

NELLIE gets to her knees and spits.

NELLIE   What the – what the fuck happened to yous? I was only gone three months.

AGGIE is panting, in pain and angry.

AGGIE   You're full of shit, Nellie Murray. Always – always have been. Don't you get it? Peace is the coward's way out. It's disgusting. It dishonours those who've given their lives for this country. It dishonours their sacrifice. We can't give up now. We have to win and crush those who fought against us. Or what was the point? What was the point of all this – this suffering?

NELLIE wipes blood from her lip. She gets slowly to her feet. She looks from AGGIE and HELEN but sees nothing familiar. She puts her fists into her eyes. She will not cry.

A beat.

She scoops a loose brick from the pavement, weighs it in her hands. AGGIE shrinks back but NELLIE hurls the brick through the window of the factory. The sound of smashing glass. She roars.

NELLIE moves off down the street and out of sight.

20.

GERTRUDE is sitting on a park bench. She is thin and drawn.

A couple walk by, arm in arm.

GERTRUDE **That should be us, Harry. You and me. Out for a stroll, not a care in the world. It's how it used to be isn't it? Back in the day when the world was the right way up and you used to hold my hand.**

She smiles.

 But you wanted to do your bit, didn't you? That's how I remember you, Harry. Strong and proud. Why the hell didn't you tell me what was going on? You let me think that things would be okay. I hate you for hiding the truth from me. I hate you for making me a fool. I hate you for leaving me with a little girl, a broken heart.

She shakes her head.

> **I have to stay silent now. I have to learn to shut my mouth. I can't talk about you to anyone. I have to say goodbye without saying goodbye. And I hope one day, I'll say your name again. Harry.**
>
> **Harry. Harry. Harry.**
>
> **Harry.**
>
> **Harry.**

The couple dance a waltz. It's unlikely, impossible. Magical.

GERTRUDE gets up and walks slowly out of the park.

21.

MRS BYERS is sitting on a park bench, pulling the petals from a poppy and placing them carefully into her purse.

NELLIE enters.

NELLIE   Mum? Where have you been? I've been looking all over for you.

MRS BYERS   Here I am.

NELLIE stops in front of her.

NELLIE   Didn't I tell you to stay in the house? The police are looking for us. You can't be running around in the park.

MRS BYERS   I wasn't running around. I was sitting. Enjoying the sunshine. It's a beautiful day isn't it?

NELLIE   It's Baltic.

NELLIE holds out her mother's coat.

NELLIE   Here. You forgot your coat.

MRS BYERS   I'm fine.

NELLIE   Go on, Mum. You'll catch your death.

MRS BYERS   Very well. Very well.

MRS BYERS takes the coat and puts it on. NELLIE stands by the bench, glancing round at the passers-by.

MRS BYERS   I don't know why you have to treat me like a child, Nellie. You're always fussing. I'm perfectly capable.

NELLIE   You're not wearing any shoes.

MRS BYERS looks down. She has bare feet.

MRS BYERS   Oh.

NELLIE   For Christ's sake, Mum. How do you forget to put on your shoes?

MRS BYERS   I didn't forget. I – I must've taken them off when I went for a paddle.

NELLIE   A what?

MRS BYERS   The light on the duck pond was so bright and inviting that I thought it would be nice to put my feet in some water.

NELLIE bends down to feel MRS BYER's ankles.

NELLIE   You're soaking wet.

MRS BYERS   Don't fuss! The sun will dry me off in no time.

NELLIE takes off her coat, gets down on her knees and dries MRS BYERS ankles and feet.

NELLIE   Can't keep doing this. We're in trouble enough without you getting arrested for public indecency.

MRS BYERS   Get off me.

NELLIE   I'm almost finished.

MRS BYERS   Stop it. People are staring.

NELLIE finishes drying MRS BYERS. She plonks herself down next to her mother, wet coat in hand. She sighs.

MRS BYERS   You should worry less about me and more about yourself, Nellie. It's not me that got us into this mess is it? You and your big words. Look where it's got you. No job, no friends, and no home to go to. I know you believe in what you're doing but at what cost? You're positively grey and your hair's falling out. That husband of yours won't fancy you if there's nothing left.

NELLIE   Thanks.

MRS BYERS   Oh. Before I forget. Did the postman have anything for me?

NELLIE   *(Shakes her head.)* Were you expecting something?

MRS BYERS   A letter from your brother.

NELLIE shakes her head.

MRS BYERS   Don't say it! Don't say it! I know you disapprove of his joining up but Joe's your brother and my son. He wasn't doing it to upset you.

NELLIE   Mum.

MRS BYERS   It's a wonder he hasn't written sooner. So unlike Joe. He used to write every week. I heard at the Post Office that the mail has backed up because of the Big Push.

NELLIE   Mum.

MRS BYERS   But that can't go on forever can it? Any day now. I'm sure of it.

NELLIE throws up her hands.

NELLIE   No, Mum. Joe's letter won't get through.

MRS BYERS   What are you talking about?

NELLIE   You know it won't.

MRS BYERS   Do I?

NELLIE   How can you keep denying it? Bugger it. We
                go through this almost every day.

MRS BYERS   What?

NELLIE   Joe is dead. Two years ago. They killed him.
                The army killed him for running away.

Silence.

MRS BYERS shakes her head.

NELLIE   I know what you're going to say…

MRS BYERS   …

NELLIE   You're going to say it's not true. That Joe was
                a good boy…

MRS BYERS   He was a good boy.

NELLIE   And that he would never do something
                wicked like that…

MRS BYERS   Joe would never do anything wicked like
                that. Never.

NELLIE   That there must be some mistake…

MRS BYERS   There must be some mistake.

NELLIE   There's no mistake. You're lying to yourself.
                If only you could admit, it wouldn't be so
                bad. You could move forward. But this –

MRS BYERS slaps NELLIE.

A beat.

MRS BYERS bursts into tears.

NELLIE reaches out and takes her mother in her arms as she weeps. A moment.

NELLIE There, there… there, there. It's alright… I believe there will be a day… maybe soon, maybe not… there will be a day when justice will take hold. There will be an end to wars. Humanity will cease fighting itself. We will rise above petty and stupid rivalries. And on that day… on that day, we will remember Joe and lads like him… We will remember and feel no shame.

Church bells ring.

MRS BYERS What? What's that?

MRS BYERS wipes her eyes.

MRS BYERS Is that the church bells?

NELLIE It can't be. They've not rung since war was declared. No – it couldn't be, could it – I don't believe it –

NELLIE jumps up. A small crowd enter the park, cheering and shouting. NELLIE grabs a passer-by.

NELLIE Excuse me. What's going on?

PASSER-BY Haven't you heard? The Yanks have joined the war.

NELLIE What?

PASSER-BY The Americans. Brilliant isn't it? Fritz has sunk one too many merchant ships and the President says enough is enough.

NELLIE stumbles, falls back onto the bench.

NELLIE The Americans… I don't believe it.

PASSER-BY   Is she alright?

MRS BYERS   What's the matter, Nellie?

NELLIE   Peace… I thought it was peace…

PASSER-BY   Well it can't be long now can it? Cheer up!
                 We will definitely win now. The enemy will
                 be on their knees by Christmas, make no
                 mistake.

The church bells continue to ring. Union Jacks and Stars and Stripes fly.

And then a massive explosion. The Western Front. Machine guns, mortars, landmines. It's deafening.

And then, at last, silence.

22.

The Last Post is played.

23.

Morning. The postman delivers a hundred final letters. The wives, mothers, sisters and daughters open the envelopes and read the contents. It is good news. It is bad news. It is the worst news. Some press the envelopes over their hearts, gasping for breath, others tear them to tiny little pieces. One of the women crumples the paper and stuffs it into her mouth.

24.

1918. London. A comfortable sitting room in a West London house.

GERTRUDE is standing before LADY ARKWRIGHT. LADY ARKWRIGHT looks her up and down.

Slight pause.

ARKWRIGHT   Hmmm. Very well. You'll do.

GERTRUDE blinks.

GERTRUDE   Beg your pardon, Your Ladyship?

ARKWRIGHT   Let's not bother with references. I'm a very
             good judge of character. One look is sufficient.

GERTRUDE   You – you mean I got the job?

ARKWRIGHT   If you'll take it.

GERTRUDE   Oh – oh yeah. Yes I'll take it. Thank you!
             Thank you very much, Your Ladyship.

ARKWRIGHT   It's Gertrude isn't it?

GERTRUDE   That's right.

ARKWRIGHT   Well Gertrude. Your duties will be quite
             various. There are only two of us but
             unfortunately, during the war, the house has
             got quite out of sorts. Like everyone else we
             had to make do without staff. I can't say His
             Lordship ever got the hang of the dusting…

GERTRUDE   *(Smiles.)* I can see…

ARKWRIGHT   You'll be pretty much responsible for
             knocking us back into shape. That doesn't
             put you off does it?

GERTRUDE   I like hard work.

ARKWRIGHT   Good girl. I say. It was a stroke of luck
             finding you.

GERTRUDE   Thank you, Your Ladyship.

ARKWRIGHT   And you have a child is that right?

GERTRUDE   A daughter.

ARKWRIGHT   It will be lovely to have a little one around
             the house. Such a long time since we've had
             any noise about the place.

GERTRUDE   You're very kind.

ARKWRIGHT   Not at all. Was your husband in the war?

GERTRUDE nods.

ARKWRIGHT   He died in battle?

GERTRUDE hesitates.

GERTRUDE   That – that's right. The Somme.

ARKWRIGHT   How very sad. The whole country has lost so much hasn't it? We all have to work hard to put it behind us and speak no more about it.

GERTRUDE   Yes.

A beat.

ARKWRIGHT   So shall we say you start on Monday? If you and your girl come tomorrow, you'll have time to settle into your quarters over the weekend.

GERTRUDE   Very good, Your ladyship.

LADY ARKWRIGHT nods her dismissal. GERTRUDE goes.

25.

Glasgow Central Station.

NELLIE, STEPHEN and MRS BYERS are standing on the platform, small suitcases in each hand.

MRS BYERS   Where are we going, Nellie?

NELLIE   I told you.

MRS BYERS   If you had I wouldn't be asking.

NELLIE   I told you three times.

MRS BYERS   I know you like to think I don't remember anything but it's not true.

NELLIE   We're going to Liverpool. Just for a few
                  weeks. A month at most. Hopefully after that
                  we'll have enough for a passage to America.
                  Did you remember the passport I gave you?

MRS BYERS   What passport?

*NELLIE puts her suitcase down and fishes in MRS BYERS' jacket
pocket. She pulls out a passport. MRS BYERS stares at it.*

MRS BYERS   Will you look at that? Fancy. I've never seen
                  one of these before.

NELLIE   Put it in your pocket now, Mum. I had to
                  queue three days for that.

MRS BYERS   *(Looking.)* Oh no Nellie. There's been a
                  mistake. This passport doesn't belong to me.
                  It's got the wrong name.

NELLIE   That's your name.

MRS BYERS   I think I know my own name.

NELLIE   It's your new name. We've talked about
                  this. I got us new names for when we go to
                  America.

MRS BYERS   Why do I need a new name?

MRS BYERS   It's just better. Trust me.

NELLIE turns to STEPHEN. He is silent.

NELLIE   Are you alright, my darling?

STEPHEN   …

NELLIE   No need to worry. It won't be long now.

STEPHEN nods but doesn't speak.

Slight pause.

MRS BYERS   I don't know if I want to go to America. How
                  long will it take? It's very far away.

NELLIE	We can't stay here, Mum.
MRS BYERS	Glasgow is our home.
NELLIE	Not any more.
MRS BYERS	But why?
NELLIE	You know why. This place is done. America is a new start.
MRS BYERS	Isn't it dangerous to sail across the Atlantic? I hear stories. German U-Boats don't care a fig for civilian ships. We could be sunk.
NELLIE	There are no German U-Boats. The war is over.
MRS BYERS	Is it?
NELLIE	It's been over for months now.

MRS BYERS claps her hands.

MRS BYERS	But that's marvellous news! Why didn't you tell me? Joe will be on his way home. Come on! We must get back. He might already be back. Goodness he could be waiting on the doorstep right this minute. Imagine his face if he finds us gone. He'll be raging.

MRS BYERS turns to go but NELLIE grabs her.

NELLIE	No.
MRS BYERS	But Joe. We have to be at home for Joe –
NELLIE	Mum, please. Can't you bloody well –
MRS BYERS	What's going on, Nellie?

A moment.

NELLIE	I left a note. Pinned to the front door. If Joe – if he comes back he'll know where to find us.

MRS BYERS   You left a note?

NELLIE nods.

MRS BYERS   That's alright then. Be a terrible shame to
                miss him. This war has separated parents
                from their children for far too long. And
                why? What is the future without the young?

Silence.

NELLIE   Right. Come on, everyone. That's our train.

The three of them move towards the train. A cloud of steam.

                        26.

1992. A committee room in the House of Parliament.

*JANET BOOTH, early forties, from London, approaches the microphone.
She speaks very closely into it.*

JANET   Is this on? Hi. Hello. Hi.

Slight reverb. She backs off.

JANET   Sorry. Sorry I don't, I'm not used to –

A beat.

JANET   Hello. My name is Janet Booth. I'm very
                pleased to be speaking to you all today
                here in the Houses of Parliament. Thank
                you to Andrew MacKinlay MP and Julian
                Putkowski for inviting me. I – I didn't know
                that I'd be speaking. I – I'm not sure what
                I'm going to say but… erm…

Slight pause.

JANET   But when we were growing up we never
                talked about my grandfather, Harry Farr. I
                knew he'd died in the First World War but
                that was all. Last year I was going on holiday

to France and I asked my gran where Harry was buried. I wanted to see his grave. But she said he didn't have one. She said he didn't have one because Harry had been shot as a coward. None of us, the family that is, knew the details of what happened to Harry. The Court Martial papers were only released very recently. Now we know that Harry was very unwell, that he had shellshock. He'd been a brave soldier but he'd become unwell and should never have been on trial in the first place... We never talked about my grandfather when we were growing up, we never asked questions, we kept silent about it all. But today that silence ends. I'm here on behalf of my gran, Gertrude Farr, and all those other families who have been silent too long –

27.

NELLIE, MRS BYERS and GERTRUDE.

ALL   **We are going forward.**

                     You can starve us
                     put us in prison
                     kill us
                     but no matter what you do
                     our voices
                     will be heard.

                     We will be heard.
                     We will be heard.

END OF PLAY

Afterword: Voices In The Dark

Whenever I write a play, I'm always asked the same thing. Is it true? It's the most natural question in the world but when it comes I'm often left without knowing how to answer.

I had the idea for this play in 2013, when the composer Gareth Williams and I were sent to Cove Park by the National Theatre of Scotland to develop a piece of music theatre about heroism and cowardice in the First World War. I knew we wanted to explore the stories of the 306 men who were shot for military crimes – cowardice, desertion, mutiny – but I'm always interested in consequences and the connections that might lie beyond the original events.

Knowing that the first part of the trilogy (*The 306: Dawn*) would be mostly male, set as it was in the trenches of The Somme in 1916, I wanted to explore the war from a female perspective back home in Britain. It seemed a neat trick to tell the second part of the story in 1917 and the more I delved into research the more exciting that choice appeared.

1917 was a momentous year. The third year of the most cataclysmic war in history. The Russian Revolution. American soldiers arriving at the Western Front and domestically, a wave of anti-war protests staged across the UK, more particularly in Glasgow, where the Women's Peace Crusade (WPC) was founded. On Sunday 8 July 1917, the WPC organised a march on Glasgow Green which saw 14 000 people marching against the war.

***

One of the main characters from *The 306: Dawn* is Joseph Byers. He was seventeen when he joined the British Army in November 1914. Like all soldiers departing for the front,

Joseph wrote his will. I have a photocopy of it. It reads: 'In the event of my Death I give the whole of my stuff to my Sister Nellie Murray'. Joseph was executed three months later and his records were lost in bombing in the Second World War. I took this absence of information as an invitation and created a new character, a possible 'Joe', a young man from Glasgow who joined up for excitement and adventure only to be faced with the cold reality of the trenches.

When it came to continuing the story – whilst at the same time trying to tell a story that would be complete unto itself – I thought about who Joseph's sister, Nellie Murray might be. Despite the work of countless historians and a genealogist employed by the National Theatre of Scotland, neither Nellie nor any other family member has ever been located. Again this gave me the opportunity to imagine, to invent, and insert a fictional character into real events.

I read everything I could about the anti-war movement, the Women's Peace Crusade, and more generally about the experience of women in war time Glasgow. The 'Home Front' has become a cosy term, associated with 'home fires' and smiling munitionettes but for many it was indeed a 'front', a battlefield. (If there is a spiritual guide to the writing of this play, it's Sylvia Pankhurst's brilliant *The Home Front* with its depictions of working women's experience in the East End of London, as well as Sylvia's relationship to the pacifist movement. I would thoroughly recommend this book.) I became fascinated by the challenges of women's lives in war time, of how a world without men functioned, and how women's voices were at the centre of the pacifist cause.

From this research, I invented Nellie. She is an amalgam of some real anti-war protesters and my imagination. Some of the things she says were said by real women. For example, Nellie paraphrases a speech by the Glaswegian peace activist Helen Crawfurd. (I've taken one of Crawfurd's speeches and turned it into the lyrics of the opening song.)

But this is not the story of Helen Crawfurd and in the gaps of what I knew to be true I've given expression to other feelings, other thoughts, other experiences of women at that time. If you'll allow me an obvious metaphor, Nellie is a torch by which I can shine light in dark places.

A real Nellie Murray did exist – we have Joseph's will to prove it – but probably not in the way I've written. Could she have existed? I'm absolutely certain that someone like her *did* but like a lot of women's stories, it has been lost.

***

I follow the facts of Gertrude Farr's story pretty closely. She was left a widow in her early twenties with her daughter Gertie only three years old. She was refused a pension, a fact she discovered in her local Post Office. Neither Gertrude's family nor her late husband's family were either able or willing to help her financially. She was urged to keep quiet. Gertrude and Gertie were forced to sleep at a neighbour's house before she found work as a maid. Gertrude did not speak of what had happened to Harry and her daughter only discovered the truth of her father's death forty years later. It wasn't until the 1980s when the rest of the family were told what had happened.

In writing the character of Gertrude, I was aided immeasurably by her family, as well as Gertrude's own testimony which she recorded for the Imperial War Museum. I had lengthy conversations with Gertrude's granddaughter, Janet Booth, and her daughter Rachel. I'd like to take this opportunity to thank them for speaking to me and generously permitting me to tell their family's story.

***

My daughter was born a few weeks before I started writing this play and I have no real memory of the process at all. Like all new parents I was overwhelmed and exhausted but I had a deadline so somehow, in the brief moments of pause and sleep, I managed to get this play onto the page. I honestly don't remember when I started it or when I finished. When I read it over and we started the journey towards production, I felt that my forgetting was mirrored by the character of Mrs Byers. (As with Nellie, we have no idea what happened to the rest of family. This play's thesis is that they changed their names and moved away.) She has forgotten Joe's death but perhaps more interestingly, she has *chosen* to forget it. It may not be willed but her brain has decided that it cannot face the truth. In Mrs Byers, I wanted to show how the war existed not only in the trenches but also in the minds of all who were affected by it and those shocks could reverberate for years, decades... even centuries.

OE April 2017.

Acknowledgements

A big thank you to Jackie, Caroline, Anna, George, Pam, Margaret-Anne, and Eileen and everyone at the National Theatre of Scotland. Thank you to John and Robert at Red Note Ensemble, everyone at Perth Horsecross and the brilliant team at Stellar Quines. Thank you to 14:18 NOW. Thank you to the actors who helped develop an earlier version of the text: Chloe Ann Tylor, Lila Clements, Joyce Henderson, and David Carlyle. Thank you to John Beales. Thank you to Sam Tranter, my excellent researcher, and to Jerry Degroot, my historical consultant. Thank you to my agents, Giles and Jen. Thank you to George and everyone at Oberon. Thank you to Katie Holt for the Russian, Tom Crawley for the German, Johnny McKnight for the Glaswegian. Thank you to my students at St Andrews. Thank you to my generous friends who read the script and told me what was missing: Lu Kemp, Kirsty Williams, David Leddy. Thank you to the wonderful cast and crew. Thank you to Jemima who made this play better in a multitude of ways. Thanks to GW, second time lucky. Thank you to my family – Emanuels, Beesleys, Cains, Maginns – and lastly thank you to VB and Matilda, my fighting women.